Lessons About Dinosaurs

By Carmel Reilly

T0342819

Contents

A Long Time Ago

Dinosaurs lived a very long time ago.

People did not live at the same time as dinosaurs.

Today, fossils teach us lessons about dinosaurs.

Fossils are bones and prints left in old rocks.

dinosaur fossil

Big and Small

Some dinosaurs were as big as jumbo jets.

Others were as little as cats.

Some had long necks,
and some had horns.

horns

long neck

Dinosaur Food

One group of dinosaurs
ate trees and grass.

They had flat teeth
to grind their food.

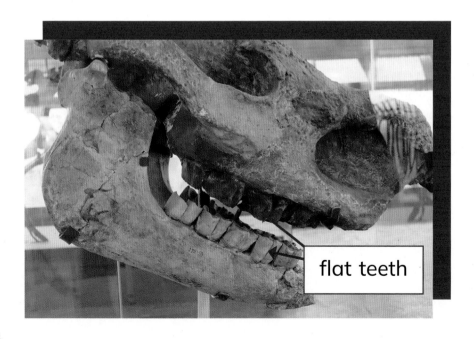

flat teeth

A second group of dinosaurs
ate meat.

They had sharp teeth
to rip up their food.

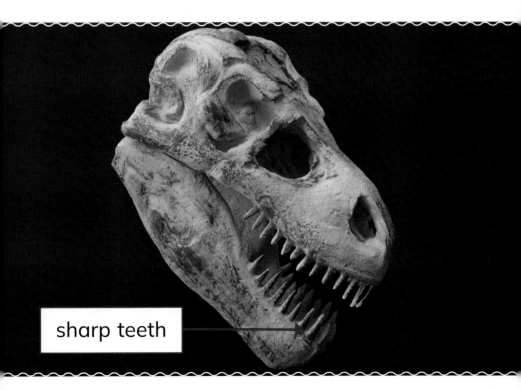

sharp teeth

Strong Back Legs

Dinosaurs had some things in common, too.

First, they had strong back legs.

back legs

Some dinosaurs walked and ran on their strong back legs.

Dinosaur Nests

The second thing dinosaurs had in common was that they laid eggs in nests.

fossil eggs

Some dinosaur nests were like bird nests.

But most dinosaurs put dirt on top of their nests.

This protected the eggs.

dinosaur nest

Digging for Dinosaurs

New dinosaur fossils
are found all the time.

They tell us a lot about
what dinosaurs were like.

This person is digging
to find a dinosaur.

If we keep digging,
we can keep learning
about dinosaurs!

CHECKING FOR MEANING

1. When did dinosaurs live? *(Literal)*

2. Which dinosaurs had sharp teeth? Why? *(Literal)*

3. Why do people want to learn more about dinosaurs? *(Inferential)*

EXTENDING VOCABULARY

ago	What is the meaning of *ago*? When is *a very long time ago*? Is this in the past or is it about to happen?
lessons	What are *lessons*? What do we hope to do when we have a lesson? What lessons do you have? What do you learn to do?
protected	What does the word *protected* mean? What is the base of this word?

MOVING BEYOND THE TEXT

1. As a class group, make a list of all the dinosaurs you know. Do you know which ones ate plants and which ones ate meat?

2. Look at some pictures of dinosaurs and talk about how they protect themselves. What special features do they have to stay safe?

3. Ask students if they have been to a dinosaur exhibit. Where are these held? Allow students to retell their experiences.

4. Allow students to draw their favourite dinosaur and write labels on their picture.

THE SCHWA

| a | e | i | o | u |

PRACTICE WORDS

ago

the

fossils

about

lessons

a

common

second

even

person